BRENT LIBRARIES	
91120000358755	
Askews & Holts	21-Feb-2018
J591.68	£12.99

ENDANGERED ANIMALS

EUROPE

by
Grace Jones

Image Credits

All images are courtesy of Shutterstock.com, unless otherwise specified. With thanks to Getty Images, Thinkstock Photo and iStockphoto. Front Cover – Ramon Carretero, Martin Mecnarowski, Holly Kuchera. 1 – Zoom Team. 4&5 – FloridaStock, DM7, Reinhold Leitner. 6&7 – Kletr, David J Martin, Patryk Kosmider, AuntSpray. 8&9 – Laborant, Ondrej Prosicky. 10&11 – miguellm, Gallinago_media, Iakov Filimonov, Victor Tyakht, zaferkizilkaya, LazyFocus, Petr Pavluvcik, photomaster, aabeele, Viktor Loki. 12&13 – Ramon Carretero, Matthew Ball, William Booth. 14&15 – Martin Mecnarowski, Erni, Philip Bird LRPS CPAGB. 16&17 – Ewais, Jan van Biljon, ESCOCIA. 18&19 – Victor Tyakht. 20&21 – zaferkizilkaya, Willyam Bradberry, StockStudio. 22&23 – Nagel Photography, MilousSK, rodimov. 24&25 – kojihirano, katatonia82, Michal Ninger. 26&27 – Lemon Tree Images, Creative Travel Projects, Karel Cerny, Monkey Business Images, Mila Supinskaya Glashchenko, Rob Wilson.

BookLife
PUBLISHING

©2018
BookLife Publishing
King's Lynn
Norfolk PE30 4LS

All rights reserved.
Printed in Malaysia.

A catalogue record for this book is available from the British Library.

ISBN: 978-1-78637-245-1

Written by:
Grace Jones

Edited by:
Kirsty Holmes

Designed by:
Drue Rintoul

CONTENTS

Page 4	**Endangered Animals**
Page 6	**Why Do Animals Become Endangered?**
Page 8	**Europe**
Page 10	**Endangered European Animals**
Page 12	**Iberian Lynx**
Page 14	**European Mink**
Page 16	**Bearded Vulture**
Page 18	**Saiga**
Page 20	**Mediterranean Monk Seal**
Page 22	**Grey Wolf**
Page 24	**Conservation Efforts in Europe**
Page 26	**How Can I Make a Difference?**
Page 28	**Find Out More**
Page 29	**Quick Quiz**
Page 30	**Glossary**
Page 32	**Index**

Words that look like this are explained in the glossary on page 30.

ENDANGERED ANIMALS

Experts estimate that there are anywhere between two million and nine million **species** living on planet Earth today, but thousands of these are in danger of dying out every single year.

What Does It Mean If a Species is Endangered?

Any species of plant or animal that is at risk of dying out completely is said to be endangered. When all individuals of a single species die, that species has become extinct. Extinction is a real possibility for all species that are already threatened or endangered. Experts estimate that between 150 and 200 different species become extinct every day.

Polar Bear

Dinosaurs are an example of an extinct species. They walked the Earth over 225 million years ago and became extinct around 65 million years ago.

The International Union for Conservation of Nature and Natural Resources (IUCN) is the main **organisation** that records which species are in danger of extinction. The species are put into different categories, from the most to the least threatened with extinction.

IUCN'S CATEGORIES OF THREATENED ANIMALS

Category	Explanation
Extinct	Species that have no surviving members
Extinct in the Wild	Species with only surviving members in **captivity**
Critically Endangered	Species that have an extremely high risk of extinction in the wild
Endangered	Species that have a high risk of extinction in the wild
Vulnerable	Species that are likely to become endangered or critically endangered in the near future
Near Threatened	Species that are likely to become vulnerable or endangered in the near future
Least Concern	Species that fit into none of the above categories

The IUCN's work is extremely important. Once a species has been recognised as endangered, organisations and **governments** will often take steps to protect the species and its **habitats** in order to save it from extinction. The practice of protecting or conserving a species and its habitats is called conservation.

The Javan rhinoceros has been categorised by the IUCN as 'critically endangered', with around 46–66 individuals remaining in the wild.

WHY DO ANIMALS BECOME ENDANGERED?

Over the last 100 years, the human **population** of the world has grown by over 4.5 billion people. As the population has grown, the damage humans do to the **environment** and wildlife has increased too. Many experts believe that human activity is the biggest threat to animals around the world today.

HABITAT DESTRUCTION

The biggest threat species face is the loss of their habitats. Large areas of land are often used to build **settlements** to provide more housing, food and **natural resources** for the growing world population. This can often destroy natural habitats, which nearby wildlife need in order to survive.

To use land for housing or farming, all the trees must be cut down and cleared from the area. This is called **deforestation**.

Pollution

Pollution is the introduction of harmful waste to the air, water or land. Pollution threatens wildlife all over the world; for example, people drop litter, which can cut, choke or even poison animals.

THE WORLD WIDE FUND FOR NATURE (WWF) ESTIMATES THAT BETWEEN 200 AND 2,000 SPECIES OF ANIMAL BECOME EXTINCT EVERY SINGLE YEAR.

Hunters and Poachers

Many species are endangered because of hunting or **poaching**. Humans throughout history have hunted certain species of animal for their meat, furs, skins or tusks.

Male African elephants are hunted by poachers for their huge tusks, which are made from a natural material called ivory and are sold for lots of money.

The dodo was a species of bird that was hunted to extinction. The last time a dodo was seen alive was in 1662.

NATURAL CAUSES

While the most serious threats to animals are caused by humans, there are natural threats to animals too. For example, it is thought that the extinction of the dinosaurs was caused by a natural event, when a **meteorite** hit the Earth. Other species may become extinct because they are not as well **adapted** to survive in their environments as others. Experts believe that the number of species that become extinct due to human activity is around 1,000 times more than those becoming extinct through natural causes.

EUROPE

Europe is one of the seven continents of the world. Continents are large areas of land that, along with five oceans, cover the Earth. The other six continents are: Africa, Antarctica, Asia, Australia, North America and South America. Europe is the second smallest continent in the world. It is located to the north of Africa and to the west of Asia. There are two oceans around the European coastline. The Arctic Ocean lies to the north of Europe and the Atlantic Ocean to the west. The east of Europe is joined by land to Asia.

CONTINENTS OF THE WORLD

DO YOU KNOW WHICH CONTINENT YOU LIVE IN?

ARCTIC OCEAN

NORTH AMERICA

ATLANTIC OCEAN

EUROPE

ASIA

PACIFIC OCEAN

PACIFIC OCEAN

SOUTH AMERICA

AFRICA

INDIAN OCEAN

AUSTRALIA

ANTARCTIC OCEAN

ANTARCTICA

FACTS ABOUT EUROPE

FACTFILE

Population: Over 739 million people.

Land Area: Over 9.9 million square kilometres (km).

Countries: 50

Highest Peak: Mount Elbrus in Russia rises to 5,643 metres (m) above **sea level**.

Longest River: The Volga river is the longest river in Europe and it is over 3,500 km long.

Biggest Country by Area: Russia. Although Russia is part of both Europe and Asia, the European part (at nearly 4 million square km) is still the biggest country in Europe.

Languages: There are 23 languages spoken in Europe.

Volga River, Russia

WILDLIFE AND HABITATS

There are many different types of habitat found across the European continent, including woodlands, wetlands, **urban** and **marine** habitats. Europe is also home to over 1,000 different species of native mammals, birds, reptiles and amphibians, and at least 155 of these are classified as threatened. **Conservationists** believe that around 16 of these are extremely likely to become extinct very soon.

There are over 223 different types of habitat found in Europe.

ENDANGERED EUROPEAN ANIMALS

While Europe has one of the smallest land masses of any continent, it has the third-biggest population size of any continent. Because of the large (and growing) European population, the single biggest threat that wildlife in Europe face is from human activity. The effects of deforestation, pollution and growing cities threaten animals across Europe.

10 ANIMALS IN DANGER IN EUROPE

1

Iberian Lynx

Conservation Status:
Endangered

Number:
Around 156 adults in the wild

2

European Mink

Conservation Status:
Critically Endangered

Number:
Unknown

3

Bearded Vulture

Conservation Status:
Near Threatened

Number:
Around 1,300–6,700 adults living in the wild

4

Saiga

Conservation Status:
Critically Endangered

Number:
Around 18,000 adults in the wild

5
Mediterranean Monk Seal

Conservation Status:
Endangered

Number:
Between 350-450 adults in the wild

6
Grey Wolf

Conservation Status:
Least Concern

Number:
Unknown

7
Sharp-Ribbed Salamander

Conservation Status:
Near Threatened

Number:
Unknown

8
European Pond Turtle

Conservation Status:
Near Threatened

Number:
Unknown

9
Rosalia Alpina

Conservation Status:
Vulnerable

Number:
Unknown

10
Italian Tree Frog

Conservation Status:
Least Concern

Number:
Unknown

IBERIAN LYNX

FACTFILE

Number Living in the Wild: Around 156 adults

IUCN Status: Endangered

Scientific Name: *Lynx pardinus*

Weight: 9-14 kilograms (kg)

Size: 88-100 centimetres (cm) long

Life Span: Around 13 years

Habitat: Mediterranean woodlands and scrublands

Diet: Carnivore

Iberian Lynx

Where Do They Live?

The Iberian Lynx lives in woodlands and scrublands along the Iberian peninsula, which is a mountainous area in the countries of Spain and Portugal. However, it is thought that very few Iberian lynxes, if any, remain in Portugal.

Key
- Oceans and Seas
- Land
- Iberian Lynx Habitats

SPAIN

12

WHY ARE THEY IN DANGER?

In recent years, large–scale deforestation has occurred in Iberian lynx habitats. It is estimated that over 80% of the Iberian lynx's habitat was destroyed between 1960 and 1990. Iberian lynx numbers have also suffered because numbers of their main **prey**, rabbits, have also declined. This has left the species with less and less food to eat. The number of rabbits has decreased because of deadly diseases like **myxomatosis**.

A Wild Rabbit Suffering From Myxomatosis

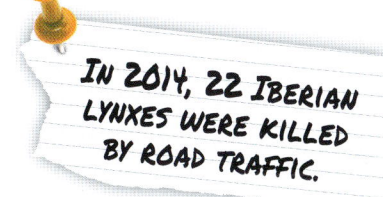

How Are They Being Protected?

Conservation efforts have focused on **breeding** Iberian lynxes in captivity with the hope of reintroducing members back into the wild. So far, over 270 individuals have been successfully bred in captivity and many of these are already back in the wild today. A conservation organisation called LIFE–Lince is planning to reintroduce Iberian lynx populations across Spain and Portugal. They also want to increase rabbit numbers, to make sure that the Iberian lynx numbers can continue to increase.

In 2014, 22 Iberian lynxes were killed by road traffic.

EUROPEAN MINK

FACTFILE

Number Living in the Wild: Unknown

IUCN Status: Critically Endangered

Scientific Name: *Mustela lutreola*

Weight: Between 600–1,000 grams (g)

Size: Between 35–58 cm long

Life Span: Up to 12 years in captivity

Habitat: They are usually found within 100 m of fresh water, on the banks of rivers, streams and lakes.

Diet: Carnivore

European Mink

Where Do They Live?

A century ago, European minks lived throughout the continent. Now, they live in and around the waterways of parts of Spain, France and Eastern Europe.

Key
- Oceans and Seas
- Land
- European Mink Habitats

EUROPE

Why Are They in Danger?

Hunting is one of the main reasons European mink populations have decreased. Over the last century, European minks have been hunted for their valuable furs. Hunting has since been made **illegal**, but European mink numbers have never recovered. In the 1920s, the American mink species was introduced to the European mink's habitat. Because the two species eat the same food, the American mink has left the European mink with less food to eat and fewer habitats in which they can live.

European mink populations have declined by 90% since the beginning of the 20th century.

HOW ARE THEY BEING PROTECTED?

In 1992, a conservation programme called European Mink EEP began with the aim of breeding European minks in captivity. There are currently around 250 members in captivity and conservationists hope to reintroduce many of these back into the wild. There are also conservation efforts underway in Estonia to home populations of European minks in new locations on the Estonian islands of Hiiumaa and Saaremaa in order to save the species from future extinction.

BEARDED VULTURE

FACTFILE

Number Living in the Wild: Around 1,300–6,700 adults

IUCN Status: Near Threatened

Scientific Name: *Gypaetus barbatus*

Weight: Between 5–7 kg

Size: Around 2.7 m

Life Span: Up to 40 years in captivity

Habitat: Mountainous areas that are usually 1,000 m above sea level

Diet: Carnivore

Bearded vultures also live in parts of Africa and Asia.

Where Do They Live?

Bearded vultures live in mountainous areas that are usually 1,000 m above sea level, in southern European countries such as France, Switzerland, Italy, Austria, Slovenia and Germany.

Key
- Oceans and Seas
- Land
- Bearded Vulture Habitats

EUROPE

WHY ARE THEY IN DANGER?

Throughout the last century, bearded vultures were hunted and killed because farmers thought they were killing their **livestock**. The main threat for this species now comes from the illegal use of poisoned **bait**. Often, farmers will lay down poisoned bait to kill animals that are thought to be pests, such as wolves, foxes, jackals and crows. However, bearded vultures will often eat the poisoned bait and die as a result.

How Are They Being Protected?

Conservation measures to save the bearded vulture have focused on 'captive breeding' programmes. These have been very successful and many members have been reintroduced back into the wild in areas such as Austria, France, Italy and even the Alps. Future conservation efforts hope to tackle the use of poisoned baits by creating new laws and strengthening existing ones.

BEARDED VULTURES HAVE STARTED TO BREED AGAIN IN ANDALUSIA.

SAIGA

FACTFILE

Number Living in the Wild: Around 18,000 adults

IUCN Status: Critically Endangered

Scientific Name: *Saiga tatarica*

Weight: 20-50 kg

Life Span: Usually between 6-10 years in the wild

Habitat: Grasslands, savannas, scrublands and deserts

Diet: Herbivore

Saiga

Where Do They Live?

Saigas are a type of antelope that are found in south-eastern parts of Europe. Numbers of Saigas in Europe have slowly decreased as they have spread further east into many parts of Asia.

Key
- Oceans and Seas
- Land
- Saiga Habitats

EUROPE

Why Are They in Danger?

The number of saigas has declined in the last 20 years because of illegal hunting. Male saigas are hunted for their valuable horns. They are sold on to be used in traditional Chinese medicine as they are thought to help cure many different illnesses. This reason, combined with habitat loss, has caused the number of saigas to decrease by around one million in the last 40 years.

Male saigas, like this one here, are often hunted for their valuable horns.

HOW ARE THEY BEING PROTECTED?

The **trade** of saiga horns, and the hunting of saigas, is illegal in many of their habitats. Despite this, illegal hunting is still extremely common. If illegal hunting is to be stopped, countries need to work together to **enforce** the law and increase the level of protection saigas currently have. Saiga Conservation Alliance, a conservation organisation, is working with the police to protect saigas from poachers as part of an international conservation plan.

MEDITERRANEAN MONK SEAL

FACTFILE

Number Living in the Wild: Between 350-450 adults

IUCN Status: Endangered

Scientific Name: *Monachus monachus*

Weight: Around 300 kg

Size: Around 2.4 m long

Life Span: Between 20-30 years in the wild

Habitat: Marine habitats

Diet: Carnivore

Mediterranean Monk Seal

Where Do They Live?

There used to be large populations of Mediterranean monk seal in the Black Sea, the Mediterranean Sea and in North Atlantic waters. Now they only live in the Mediterranean Sea, along the coasts of Greece, Cyprus and western and southern Turkey.

Key
- Oceans and Seas
- Land
- Monk Seal Habitats

EUROPE

WHY ARE THEY IN DANGER?

For hundreds of years, Mediterranean monk seals have been hunted for their furs and meat. Now the species is threatened because their marine habitats are being damaged and destroyed. Mediterranean monk seals used to raise and give birth to their young on open stretches of beach. However, because of **urban development**, they can no longer use these and have been forced to give birth in caves where they are safe from humans. More than half of seal pups don't live longer than two months because they are washed away or drowned when storms hit their cave.

In 1997, it was thought that a fatal virus was responsible for the deaths of over two thirds of the largest surviving monk seal population at Cabo Blanco off the coastline of Western Sahara, Africa.

How Are They Being Protected?

Conservation action has focused on protecting breeding caves, stopping damaging fishing methods and protecting beach habitats. Government funding from different countries has also been used to study the current population and to educate people on the importance of conserving the seals. Conservation efforts over the last 30 years have led to a small increase in the monk seal population. Further conservation steps need to be taken in order to save the Mediterranean monk seal from extinction.

THE MEDITERRANEAN MONK SEAL IS ONE OF THE MOST ENDANGERED SEAL SPECIES ON THE PLANET.

GREY WOLF

FACTFILE

Number Living in the Wild: Unknown

IUCN Status: Least Concern

Scientific Name: *Canis lupus*

Weight: Between 25-65 kg

Size: Between 1.3-1.9 m long

Life Span: Between 7-10 years in the wild

Habitat: Woodlands, forests, grasslands, deserts and tundra

Diet: Carnivore

Grey wolves also live in North America and Asia.

Where Do They Live?

Grey wolves used to live all over Europe. They no longer live in Western Europe and have disappeared from many other European countries where they used to be found. Grey wolves are well adapted to live in many different types of habitat found across the continent including woodlands, forests, grasslands, deserts and tundra.

Key

- Oceans and Seas
- Land
- Grey Wolf Habitats

EUROPE

Why Are They in Danger?

The **range** of the grey wolf is around one third of what it used to be. The biggest threat to grey wolves is from humans. Grey wolves are often thought to kill and eat farmers' livestock and are sometimes believed to be dangerous to humans. For these reasons, they are often killed by poisoning, shooting and **trapping**.

HOW ARE THEY BEING PROTECTED?

The international conservation organisation, WWF, is trying to resolve the human–wildlife **conflict** that is responsible for many grey wolf deaths every single year. They are listening to the concerns of local farmers and people, with the hope of helping them and, in turn, saving the grey wolf from being killed. The WWF are also studying wolves to discover the best methods for future protection and save them from extinction.

CONSERVATION EFFORTS IN EUROPE

Many steps have already been taken to protect wildlife and conserve habitats throughout Europe, but much more can still be done to save endangered animals from extinction.

Education

Education is the one of the most important tools we have to help animals that are at risk. Education about the wildlife around us, and the important part it plays within our world, can often be enough to change negative attitudes. One example of this is the campaign for the Mediterranean monk seal. Teaching people about the seals can reduce the damage caused to the seals' habitats from tourists and fishing.

LAWS AND GOVERNMENTS

Much progress has been made to legally protect European wildlife. Despite this, illegal hunting still occurs. Often, even if it is illegal to hunt animals, the law is not followed and the people who break the law might never be caught or punished. For animals such as the saiga or the grey wolf, who are often illegally hunted, their future survival depends on countries working together to make sure that illegal hunting is stopped.

According to the IUCN, up to 25% of European animal species are now facing extinction.

Wildlife tourists, like these ones here at Berlin Zoological Garden, can help to protect wildlife and conserve habitats around the world.

WILDLIFE TOURISM

Many wildlife organisations, charities and governments around the world are using the money that is made from **wildlife tourism** to protect endangered animals throughout Europe. The Berlin Zoological Garden in Berlin, Germany, receives more than three million visitors a year. Much of the money that they make from wildlife tourism is used to fund conservation projects throughout Europe and the rest of the world. For example, they have bred many endangered European species in captivity, which have successfully been released back into the wild. These include bearded vultures and European bison.

HOW CAN I MAKE A DIFFERENCE?

1 CAMPAIGN WITH AN ORGANISATION

Wildlife organisations such as WWF and Greenpeace have helped to save many endangered species and convince countries to change their laws through campaigning.

2 DONATE TO A CHARITY YOU BELIEVE IN

You can usually donate as little or as much as you want and most charities show you how your donations are helping to make a difference.

3 LEARN MORE ABOUT ENDANGERED SPECIES IN YOUR AREA

One of the most important ways to protect endangered species is by understanding the threats that they face. Visit a local wildlife refuge, national park or reserve, or join a local wildlife organisation.

4 ADOPT AN ANIMAL

Your donation will normally go to feeding and looking after the animal that you have adopted. You'll usually get an adoption certificate and regular updates on how your animal is doing.

5 HELP TO RAISE AWARENESS BY TALKING TO OTHERS

It is important that we all talk about issues that may threaten wildlife throughout the world. By talking about these issues, it can help to make people aware of how they may be affecting wildlife and how they can help.

6 VOLUNTEER AT A LOCAL WILDLIFE CHARITY OR SHELTER

It is not only endangered animals who need our help; we should help to care for all the animals in the world.

FIND OUT MORE

To find out more about endangered species in Europe and what you can do to get involved with conservation efforts, visit:

Berlin Zoological Garden
www.zoo-berlin.de/en

International Union for Conservation of Nature (IUCN)
www.iucnredlist.org

Saiga Conservation Alliance (SCA)
www. saiga-conservation.org

World Wide Fund for Nature (WWF)
www.worldwildlife.org

To discover more about other endangered animals around the world take a look at more books in this series:

Antarctica, Endangered Animals
Grace Jones (BookLife, 2018)

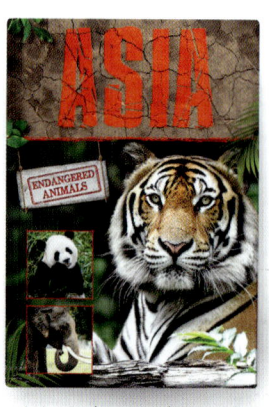

Asia, Endangered Animals
Grace Jones (BookLife, 2018)

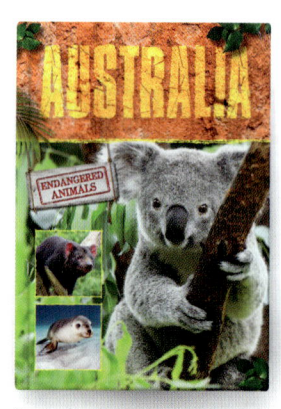

Australia, Endangered Animals
Grace Jones (BookLife, 2018)

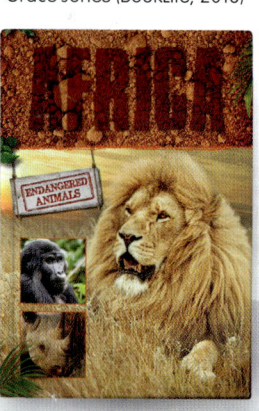

Africa, Endangered Animals
Grace Jones (BookLife, 2018)

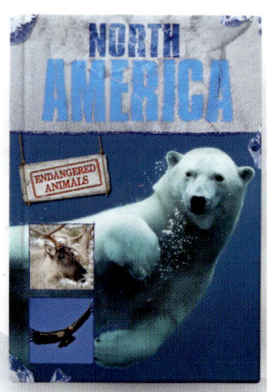

North America, Endangered Animals
Grace Jones (BookLife, 2018)

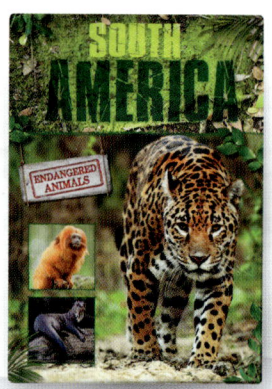

South America, Endangered Animals
Grace Jones (BookLife, 2018)

QUICK QUIZ

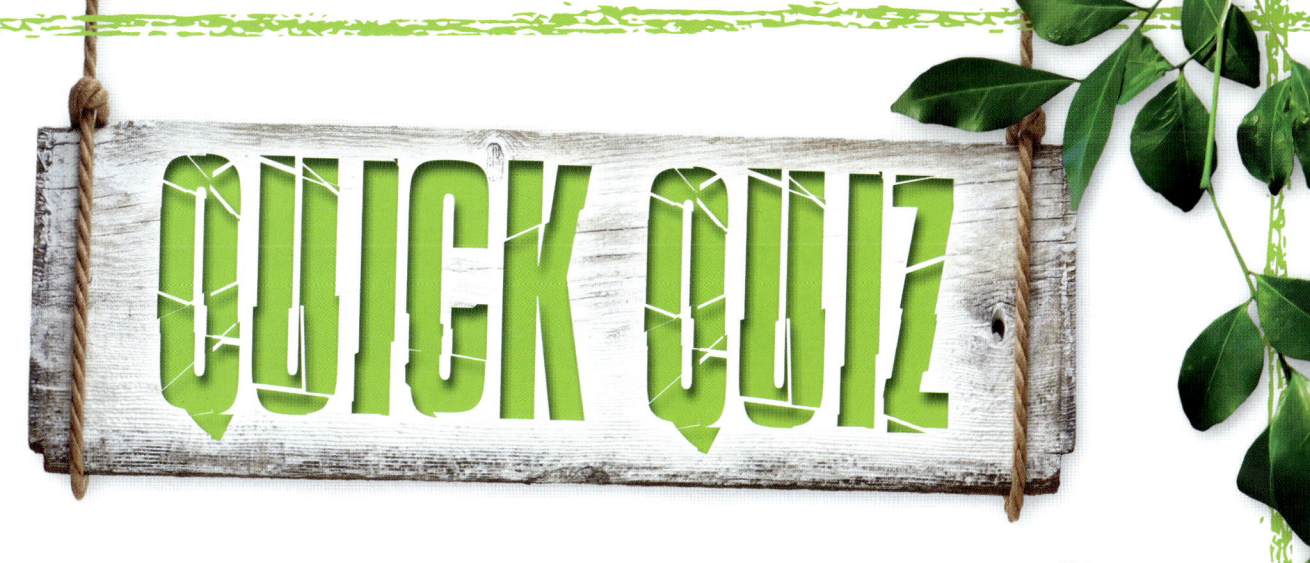

1. HOW MANY MEDITERRANEAN MONK SEALS ARE LIVING IN THE WILD?

2. WHAT IS THE SCIENTIFIC NAME OF THE GREY WOLF?

3. WHICH HABITATS DO SAIGAS LIVE IN?

4. HOW MUCH DO IBERIAN LYNXES WEIGH?

5. HOW LONG DO BEARDED VULTURES USUALLY LIVE FOR?

6. WHAT IS THE IUCN CONSERVATION STATUS OF THE EUROPEAN MINK?

For answers see the bottom of page 32.

GLOSSARY

adapted	changed over time to suit different conditions
bait	food used to attract animals as prey
breeding	the process of producing young
captivity	animals that are cared for by humans and not living in the wild
carnivore	animals that eat other animals rather than plants
conflict	active disagreements
conservationists	people who act for the protection of wildlife and the environment
deforestation	the action of cutting down trees on large areas of land
enforce	to make someone or a group of people to follow a law or rule
environment	the natural world
habitats	the natural environments in which animals or plants live
herbivore	an animal that only eats plants
governments	groups of people with the authority to run countries and decide their laws
illegal	forbidden by law
livestock	animals that are kept for farming purposes
marine	relating to the sea

meteorite	a piece of rock that successfully enters a planet's atmosphere without being destroyed
myxomatosis	an infectious disease that affects rabbits
natural resources	useful materials that are created by nature
organisation	an organised group of people who work together for a shared purpose
poaching	the act of the illegal capturing or killing of wild animals
population	the number of people living in a place
prey	animals that are hunted by other animals for food
range	the area in which a species can be found
savannas	flat areas of land covered with grass and with few trees
scrublands	lands with shrubs or small trees on them
sea level	the level of the sea's surface
settlements	places people live permanently, like villages or towns
species	a group of very similar animals or plants that are capable of producing young together
trade	to buy and sell goods
trapping	the act of catching animals, usually with a trap
tundra	large, flat areas of frozen, treeless lands in the Arctic regions of Europe, Asia and North America
urban	relating to a city or town
urban development	the construction of new buildings and houses
wildlife tourism	the actions and industry behind attracting people to visit new places to see wildlife

INDEX

A
American minks 15
Arctic Ocean 8
Atlantic Ocean 8
Asia 8-9, 16, 18, 22

B
baits 17
bearded vultures 10, 16-17, 25, 29
Berlin Zoological Garden 25

C
captivity 5, 13-16, 25
Chinese medicines 19
coastlines 8, 20-21
conservationists 9, 15
continents 8-10, 14, 22

D
deforestation 6, 10, 13
deserts 18, 22
dinosaurs 4, 7
diseases 13

E
education 21, 24
Estonia 15
European minks 10, 14-15
European pond turtles 11
extinction 4-5, 7, 15, 21, 23-24

F
farming 6, 17, 23
fishing 21, 24
forests 6, 10, 13, 22
France 14, 16-17
furs 7, 15, 21

G
governments 5, 21, 25
grey wolves 11, 22-24

H
habitat destruction 5-6, 13, 19, 21, 24
horns 19
hunting 7, 15, 17, 19, 21, 24

I
Iberian lynxes 10, 12-13
Italian tree frogs 11
IUCN 5, 12, 14, 16, 18, 20, 22, 24

L
lakes 14
laws 17, 19, 24, 26
LIFE-lince 13
livestock 17, 23

M
Mediterranean monk seals 11, 20-21, 24
Mediterranean sea 20
mountains 12, 16
myxamatosis 13

P
poaching 7
pollution 6, 10
Portugal 12-13

R
rabbits 13, 14
rivers 9
Rosalia alpinas 11
Russia 9

S
Saiga Conservation Alliance 19, 28
saigas 10, 18-19, 24
savannas 18
settlements 6
scrublands 12, 18
sharp-ribbed salamanders 11
Spain 12-14
streams 14

W
wetlands 9
wildlife tourism 25
woodlands 9, 12, 22
WWF 6, 23, 26

1. Between 350–450 adults in the wild **2.** Canis Lupus **3.** Grasslands, savannas, scrublands and deserts
4. Between 9 – 14 kilograms **5.** Up to 40 years in captivity **6.** Critically Endangered